ONE HEART

written by
Farzaneh Ghadirian

ONE HEART/Farzaneh Ghadirian **1st Edition**
ISBN 978-0-6456495-7-4

This book belongs to

_____

Dedicated to
all the children
of the world

Once upon a time,

somewhere far, far away,

there was a big, black hole

sitting alone in a vast, empty space.

That big black hole
created a universe
filled with galaxies
and energy.

In those galaxies,

there are solar systems, asteroids, and even comets.

In the solar system we call home,

there are many planets.

Ours even has a big, round moon.

Along with a big, round moon
is a giant, bright Sun.
Floating between everything,
there is ice and space rocks.

MOON

EARTH

Circling the giant, bright Sun,

there are eight planets.

One of those planets is the place where we live,

and it is called Earth.

The Earth, our planet, has a massive blue sky.

In that blue sky, there are velvety clouds.

Near the clouds, there are flying birds.

Rising up from the land, there are mountains and hills.

On top of the mountains, there are rocks and fossils.

Deep down in the earth,

there are rivers and seas.

In these waters, there are marine creatures

like fish and crabs, whales and eels.

Deep in the jungles,

there are animals and trees.

Among all the trees, there is wildlife

like tigers and chimpanzees.

Expanding out a little further,

there are **seven continents** and their countries.

In each country, there are roads and cities

with parks, buildings, and natural settings.

Greenland

Europe

Asia

North
America

South
America

Africa

Australia

Antarctica

In those buildings, there are people living.

Within those walls, parents are thinking...

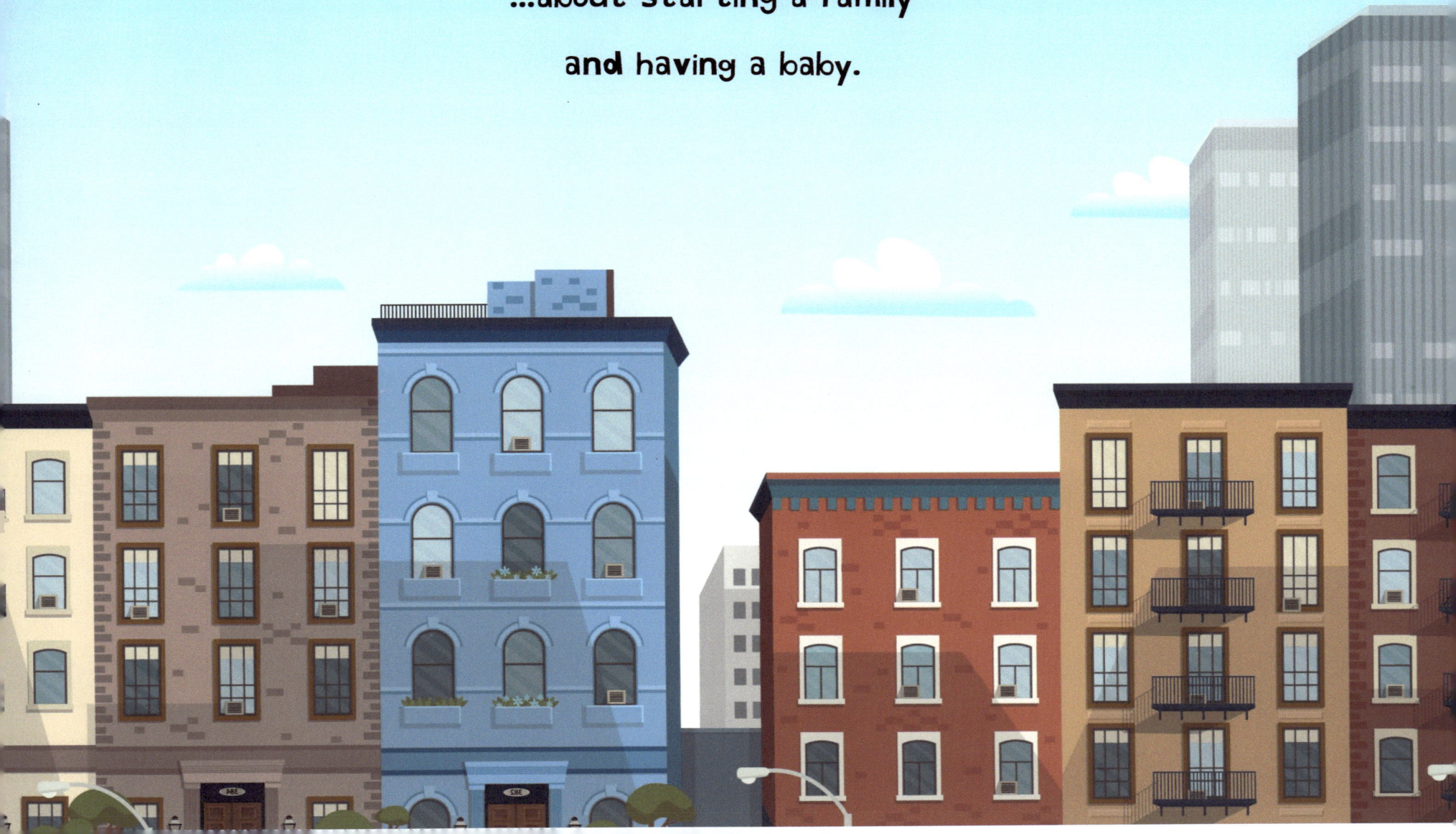

...about starting a family

and having a baby.

In a mummy's tummy,

a little organ is developing.

That little organ, the heart,

starts growing.

While the heart is growing, the baby is forming.

As the baby is forming, mummy's tummy starts expanding.

While mummy's tummy expands, the baby continues evolving.

While the baby is evolving, there are more organs developing.

While the organs are developing,

days and nights keep passing.

While the days and nights are passing,

the baby's heart is beating.

While the baby's heart is beating, the universe is vibrating.

While the universe is vibrating, the baby's heart continues forming.

As the baby's heart is forming, the universe is creating.

As the universe keeps creating, the baby's body continues shaping.

And then, the day comes when a baby is born.

Maybe a boy

or maybe a girl.

It could be you!

From the baby's heart to the mummy's tummy,

from the parents' house to the giant city,

from the city to the country to the continent,

from the continent filled with

jungles, rivers, and seas

to the sky, the moon, and the sun,

COMET

SUN

MERCURY

VENUS

EA

COMET

COMET

COMET

MARS

VENUS

NEPTUNE

MERCURY

MOON

URANUS

SUN

Earth

JUPITER

SATURN

CO

SUN

PLUTO

COMET

from the sun to the stars, planets, and all the galaxies,

they are all moving and motivating,

stimulating and creating.

MESSAGE OF
LOVE

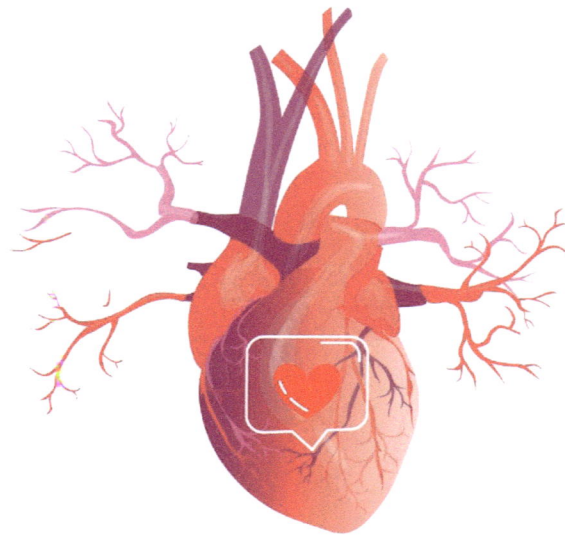

They are sending a message to your heart

that the universe's foundation has been shaped by love

and that love has been implanted into your heart.

And your heart can spread that love –
love for yourself and love to others,
to all in any shapes and colours.

SPREADING
LOVE

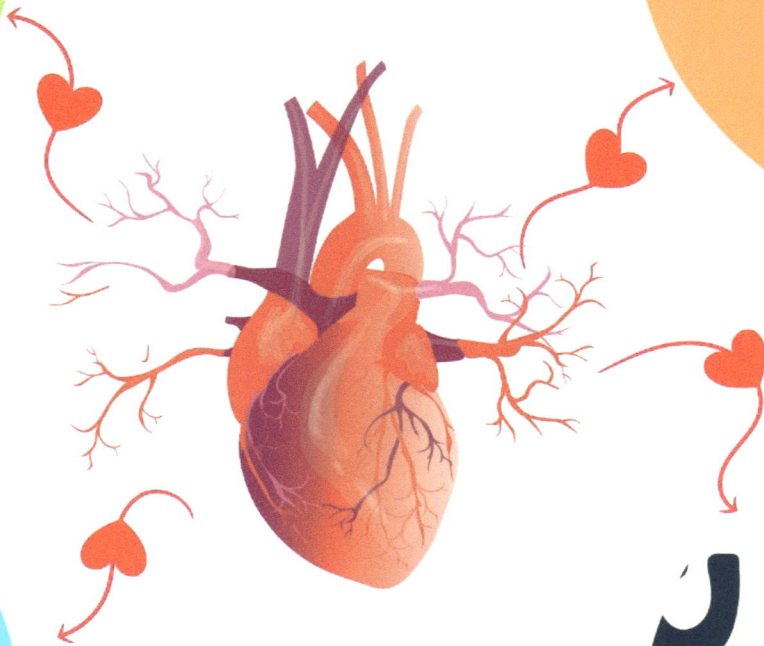

YOUR SELF

SPREADING LOVE

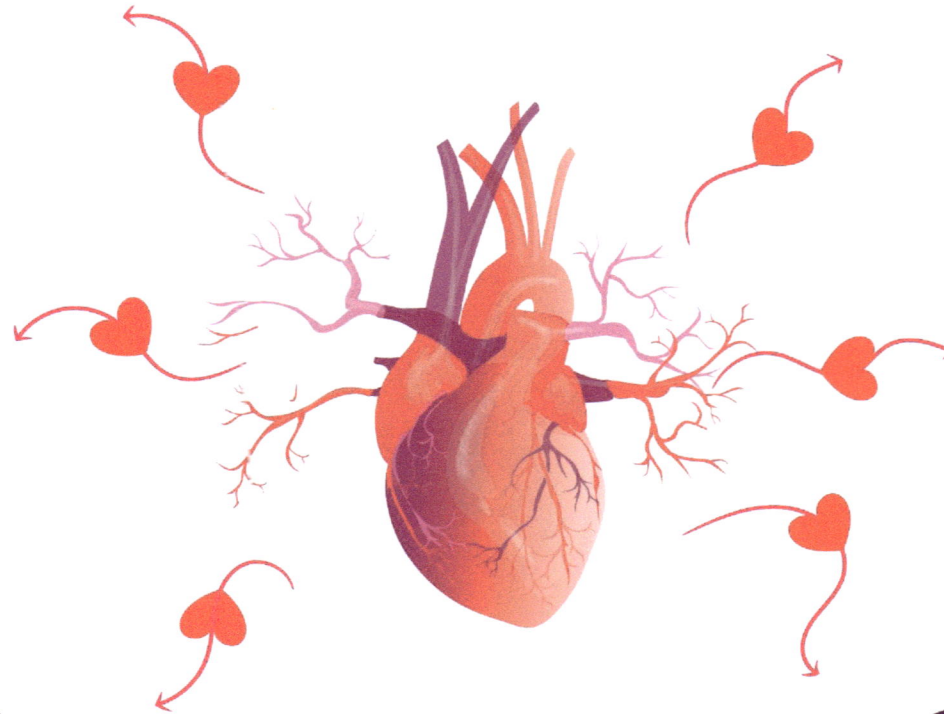

Love to the earth and to the moon.

Love to the Sun and to the shooting stars.

Love to all creatures, big or small,

living in the jungles or the seas.

Wherever you go and whatever you see,

we are all connected, up to down and in-between.

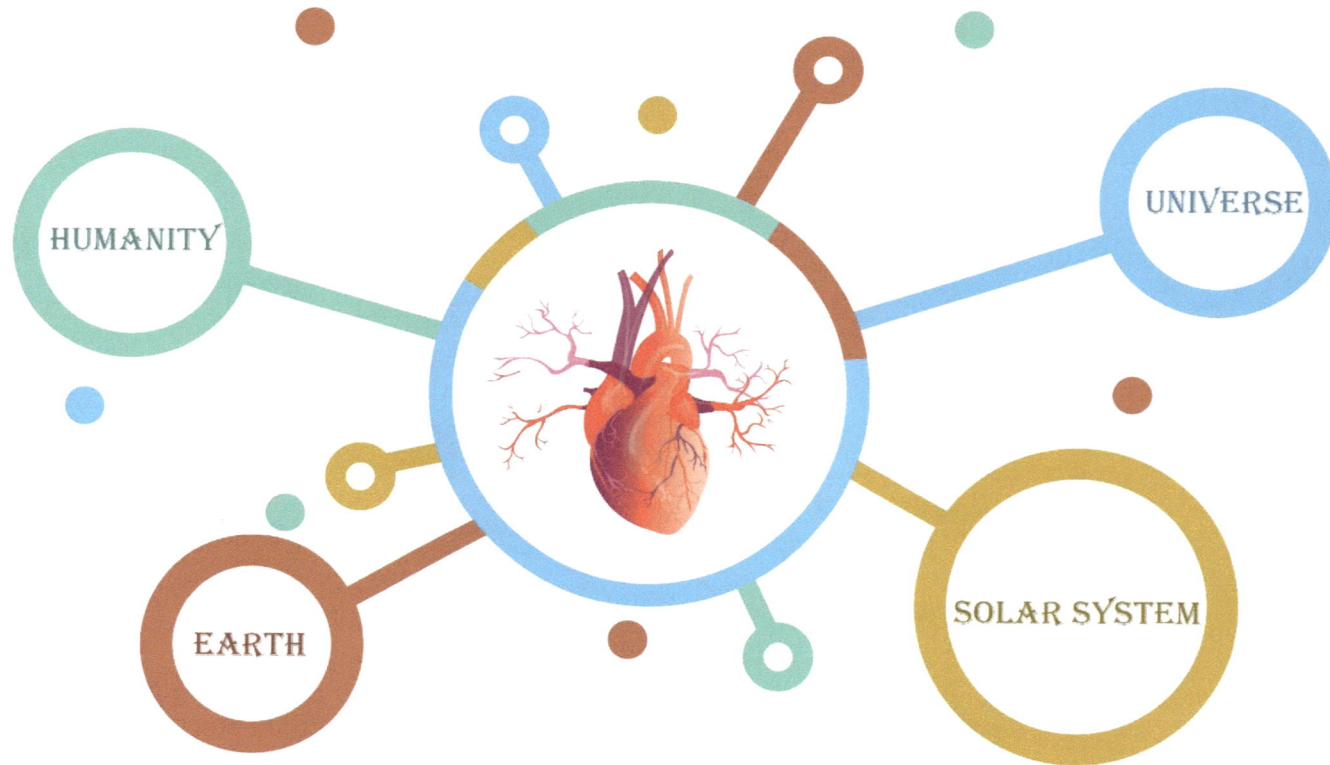

Do you know the purpose of living?

To match the beat of the universe to your heartbeat!

THE END

About the Author

Farzaneh Ghadirian migrated to Australia over twenty years ago. She enjoys reading books. She wrote her very first book when she was eight years old. Her parents' storeroom was where she set up the library. She never thought that she would be a writer one day, but with self-healing and self-realisation, she returned to her childhood passion and started writing again.

www.ingramcontent.com/pod-product-compliance
Lightning Source LLC
Chambersburg PA
CBHW040711150426

42811CB00061B/1820